Safeguarding Your Collection in Travel

SAFEGUARDING YOUR COLLECTION IN TRAVEL

Caroline K. Keck

American Association for State and Local History

Nashville/1970

Printed in the United States of America

Library of Congress Catalog Card Number: 73-138325

Acknowledgements

Collecting material and illustrations for this little booklet was facilitated by the generous assistance of many people. Special appreciation is due to Miss Kay Silberfeld, Mr. Victor Covey and Mr. Joe Brinkley of the Baltimore Museum of Art; to Mr. C. R. Jones of The New York State Historical Association; and to Miss Deborah Cannon, Mrs. Irma Cizek, Mrs. Agnes Halsey Jones, Mr. Sheldon Keck and Mr. John Ryan of Cooperstown; and last but far from least to Mr. H. J. Swinney, Director of the Adirondack Museum, Blue Mountain Lake, New York.

Caroline K. Keck
Cooperstown, New York
1970

Contents

Safeguarding Your Collection in Travel

Introduction

"Every time an object is moved or handled it dies a little".* The sorry truth of this statement would be less steadily confirmed if borrowers and lenders, shippers and packers, were all better informed on the nature of risks and on the available precautions. Because major museums constantly interchange collections, most of the published instructions on how to avoid loss and damage in moving valuables apply to large well-staffed institutions. Historical societies have seldom been prone to perpetual motion for their exhibits but they have never been entirely immune from transportation worries. All have, at one time or another, been charged with arranging the arrival of donations from benefactors—and too often many of these have been received in far from anticipated state.

Today, state and local history associations are literally being forced into the travel agency business. Recognized as rich and almost untapped sources for displays at world fairs, centennials, at neighboring and distant art and history museums, they face an ever-increasing demand for loans of their prized possessions. For the small institutions, expert services are rarely accessible; they must undertake a do-it-yourself concept. Personnel, never instructed in what to watch out for and how to

*David Little, Director, Essex Institute, Salem, Massachusetts

forestall accidents, can hardly be blamed for ensuing disasters. But granted that some hazards of travel are difficult to avoid, continual damage to travelling collections is unwarranted. A concise description of the individual physical characteristics and the individual protective requirements of historic and artistic works, combined with the basic principles governing security for an object in motion, will give custodians an understanding of the job ahead. This text and the photographs which illustrate it have been planned to spare newcomers the expense and tragedies of inexperience.

Only items in sound state can withstand travel

Naturally, vulnerable items like fragile glassware and pastel paintings should avoid all travel. No object crumbling with age or neglect should travel until it has received preservation treatment. If any object is to be sent out on a trip, first attention should be directed to its physical condition. Appearances are deceiving; so are our ideas about the strength of materials. A paper document may have dried out to powdering brittleness; a framed canvas painting may be wholly or partly loose from its wooden stretcher; china, furniture, silverware, may have old repairs where formerly-strong adhesives have all but lost their joining powers. Anything lasts only as long as its parts remain stuck together. If, before considering the release of a piece in your collection, you can determine that its parts are no longer firmly united, you will forestall the inevitable additional disruption it would suffer from shocks of motion.

Space to work in

Few historic houses can assign separate permanent areas for shipping and receiving operations. All would benefit from setting aside a non-transit space for such work. Where this is simply not feasible, at least plan a portion of a large room so that it may be temporarily cleared for service. You need a strong table, a flexible light (Tensor, gooseneck lamp, or even a good flashlight), a hand magnifier, and ample unencumbered floor space to move around in. No one can work in clutter without risking accidents.

Inspecting an object

The most reliable form of physical inspection comes from the examining eye of a professional conservator. This is the only advisable precaution to take when the object about to travel is valued and rare. However, evidences of dangerous deterioration can become obvious to any intelligent viewer who has learned how to hunt for them. All that is necessary is a flexible light source and an earnest desire to find out what the object can tell you about itself.

Make sure the object is placed on a solid cleared surface which allows easy access to all its parts. Use the flexible light source as a probe to augment your weather eye: slant the beam obliquely to all surfaces, side to side, back to front. You are hunting for signs of separation, for parts which are lifted, tented, buckled out of their proper plane. If these are suddenly silhouetted by your ray of light, use a hand magnifier to see how serious the distortion may be. You may discover that some separations are ancient and firm (see Fig 1, illustrative series #4); others unbelievably fragile, vulnerable to a finger's touch. Be sure to check, especially with furniture, all joined sections. Test with caution. If you find any evidence that a slight jar would tend to shake off part of your object, do not let it travel.

Admitting that no amateur inspection can substitute for the technical examination performed by a trained conservator, and taking into account that not every form of serious disintegration in an artifact records itself on the surface, nevertheless a vast proportion of unnecessary loss can be eliminated by pre-transit investigations undertaken by a self-taught, dedicated custodian. It is gratifying how swiftly faults become apparent to a searching glance after the first few forays into detection. To omit this safeguard INVITES trouble.

Always extend inspection to include accessories

When carefully examined, corners and elaborations of carving, inner and outer moldings of frames, may be found to be weakly joined or even split apart. The relation between any frame and what it encloses can be visibly satisfactory but possess no more than token attachment. Loose nails, wires, or stretcher keys can scratch and puncture; old screw-eyes and hinges can work free or break. Secure or replace all ineffectual portions of any item before permitting travel.

Special attention must be given to all objects which include flat glass. Frame glass has been known to rest miraculously in place, its original securities long vanished. Disturbed by a jolt, glass can break and destroy what it was intended to protect. Where possible replace glass before travel with Plexiglas. (For watercolors and paintings, and all light sensitive designs, use Plexiglas UF III which is ultraviolet retarding.) When such substitution is not feasible, before packing a glazed object crisscross the glass with self-adhesive masking or decorator's tapes (Fig 1 and 2). Keep your applied tapes short of frame rims as their adhesive can pull off finishes if carelessly removed. NEVER tape Plexiglas. It is not subject to shattering and the tapes leave an irremovable residue on its surface. With natural glass the tapes are easily removed and the glass cleaned before the item is put on display. Always require similar protection of all glazed items on return shipment.

When handles, finials, and metal ornaments are por-

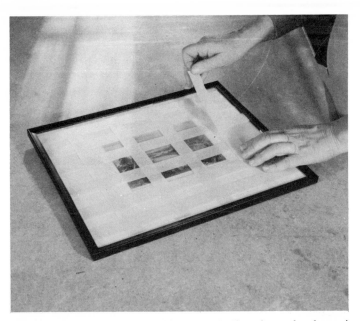

Fig 1. Applying strips of masking tape to the glass of a framed print before packing it for travel. Tapes are applied in a crisscross grid and do not extend over the frame.

tions of your loan, securing these with masking tapes risks the same loss of finish overlapping tapes do for frames. If you disengage these parts, as you would the pendulum and key of a clock, and pack them separately wrapped, be sure to note this fact prominently for the unpacker or they may be ignored, even lost. The best place to adhere this notice is on the front wrapping of the main body of your artifact. Never leave parts loose within an object. No matter how much cushioning is subsequently applied to protect an exterior, if there are free-floating inner parts, damage will result.

Photography for your record

Whenever you decide to ship out an item from your collection which is rare or valued at over $500, photograph it before packing. Date this photograph, or better yet, include the date in your negative (see illustrative series #1). Even where previous photographs exist they seldom mirror current appearances and are never accorded the same unquestioned proof of claim granted to a pre-shipment photographic record of condition.

Almost anyone can take reasonably good photographs with the equipment available on the market. Cameras and photographic lights can be borrowed. A time-saver well worth its cost is Polaroid film (black and white is adequate) type 55 P/N (currently available in 4"x5" film packets) which produces a print with its own nega-

Fig 2. This is a damage record photograph, made with Polaroid film prior to any further unpacking, when the crate was opened and the split in the frame corner observed. Subsequent examination revealed that the glass was shattered in the area adjacent to the frame break. Because the broken pieces of glass adhered to the tapes, they did not scratch or puncture the painting. It was undamaged. Direct transmission of transit blows broke the frame corner and the glass but the real culprit was the shipper who used a crate too small to permit adequate cushioning of its contents against just such travel shocks.

tive in record time and with great ease. When you are documenting an object in the round or one with detail or extra size more than one view may be necessary. In every case make sure vital characteristics of the object have been recorded in the state in which they exist.

One loss or serious damage where your record photography facilitates undisputed and prompt recompense is all that is needed to convince a board of trustees of the immense value of this slight additional expense. Without a photograph, what hope would you have of recovering the object should it be lost or stolen in travel? The first thing insurance agents and police ask for is a photograph. Take one.

Written documentation

Without secretarial help too much paper work is self-defeating. If lending from your collections develops into a major occupation, your own adaptation of examples of the examination, loan, and shipping forms (see sheets I, II, and III) used by other institutions will save time and help bolster your attention to the vast variety of detail involved. If you rarely lend, use such forms as a guide but do not try to mimeograph a reserve supply. However, it is far wiser to note down observations for reference against your own inspection of the object on its return. A written account is more reliable than memory.

Considerations before agreeing to release an object for loan

Never agree to lend any piece in your collection when your own inspection of its physical condition tells you any portion is unsound. Should the borrower be persistent tell him he will first have to pay costs for the proper preservation of the item he so badly covets. Quite often an eager borrower agrees to foot this expense. Never lend an object which you foresee might be exposed to circumstances which could render it unsound. This is harder to estimate without expertise but there are rules of thumb. Objects made of wood or with wooden parts will presumably react disastrously to excessive fluctuations of humidity. Metal items, especially those of large size and with thin portions, may distort, even break, under extremes of temperature. Textiles, paper, straw will embrittle and deteriorate if exposed to intensities of light and heat. Watercolors and dyes will fade in direct sunlight or strong fluorescent light. All delicate surfaces are apt to suffer from the effects of airborne pollutants. When you are worried about presumable damage from changed environment ask advice of a professional conservator.

Occasionally the prestige of a borrower or of his exhibition will compel an otherwise deniable loan (see illustrative series #4). In general, do not lend unless you are satisfied that your object is structurally sound, its composition will experience no appreciable damage from atmospheric changes, and—most important of all—you believe that in event of total loss you would be able to replace the item in your collection. You and your board of trustees make the final decisions; your mutual responsibility is toward the collections, the assets of your institution. They must not be allowed to depreciate needlessly.

Investigate your borrower

Once the decision has been reached to release part of your collection, the next concern is what type of care will be accorded to your possession from the time it leaves your premises until the time it returns. Is your loan departing for a single or a multiple stop exhibition? What are the conditions of display? Will your piece be guarded against vandalism or accident from a viewing public? Will it be unpacked, handled, and repacked by

competent hands? What methods of coverage are offer-
ed? Will the borrower pay costs for appropriate packaging? Unless you ask all the details in advance, YOU
are as liable as your borrower for any subsequent damage. Where guarantees are optimum and performance
turns out to be negligent, that borrower should be pil-
loried in a published "black-list" printed in your na-
tional news bulletin.* There is no better way calculated
to protect you and your colleagues from abuse, and also
to deter excessive rise in insurance rates which inevita-
bly follows excessive claims for destruction.

Do not content yourself with telephone or other word
of mouth assurances. Insist that every detail of attention
desired by you—and your board of trustees—be confirmed in written and signed statements, spelled out to
the exact letter of agreement. It is safer for your collection that you be persistently over-cautious than agreea-
bly casual. If you demand care for your possessions
you inculcate respect for them among strangers.

Principles of good packing

Packing protection for historic and artistic works is
based on "floating" the object inside a solid, water-tight,
and internally shock-absorbing crate. Good packing
depends on intelligent and skilled people. They are rare.
Facilities for prolonged carpentry on the premises are
beyond most small institutions. Shipping crates are pre-
ferably constructed to specifications by outside competent workmen and delivered to your premises for final
packing by custodial hands.

---

*Listing exact details is not necessary, a simple statement that such and such
an institution has demonstrated negligence or sub-standard performance as
a borrower is sufficient. This permits colleagues to ask further details if
they wish to learn what these were, and serves to warn them against the
culprit.

Do not entrust any piece in your collection to un-supervised packing by a commercial firm. This is a flat statement made after thirty-five years of experience in countless locales. Despite claims to the contrary, reputable firms make utterly improper crates for cultural artifacts, use harmful systems for constraint and cushioning, and invariably nail boxes, hammering them closed after your valued items are inside. For those of you who have received exactly the kind of crate described, there is no need to elaborate on how frustrating they are to open (Fig 3), risky to unpack, or how much time, effort, and money can be spent readying them and their contents for any conceivably safe return. Order crates made to specifications and fill and seal them yourself.

How to estimate specifications for a crate

Ordering your first crate from a carpenter will be an instructive experience. In the beginning almost

Fig 3. The plywood lid of this crate had been nailed down with adhesive-coated nails. To free the lid without inflicting strain on the contents required time, effort, and an assortment of heavy tools. Apart from its destructive and frustrating opening problem, a crate lid rimmed with nail ends is a hazard to personnel and to the further unpacking of its contents.

everyone makes measurement errors. If your carpenter can see what you want to ship and you explain to him that you not only want the object "floated," cushioned against external shocks, but also restrained from "shifting" during travel motion, there will be less chance for miscalculations. With his advice, the two of you can work out general design, materials to employ, and make accurate measurements.

What the carpenter needs for guidance are the three inner dimensions—height, width and depth—of the crate he must construct. These are reached by adding to the greatest dimensions of your object (1) the thickness of its initial wrappings or boxing plus (2) appropriate allowance for interior cushioning between this and the inner faces of its shipping crate. The commonest mistake is to underestimate depth.

For the newcomer, it is easier to figure crate measurements after your item has been initially wrapped or boxed. Initial wrapping with china, glassware, furniture, may involve all-over covering with tissue, cloth, or padding, or just protecting delicate extremities (see illustrative series #2). For glazed pictures with small frames, placques or flat documents, it might mean a tailored box (see illustrative series #3). The amount of additional cushioning required on all sides varies according to the fragility of the contents, the protection afforded by its initial wrapping or boxing, and the presumed strains of the travel. For padded and wrapped ceramics additional rim cushioning might run to four to six inches; for a wrapped framed painting, only two to three. The cushioning supplied around the extremities of the contents of a crate is also referred to as its "filling." Eventually you learn to figure with reasonable accuracy the inner dimensions of a crate just from studying the object itself. In early attempts, if you feel uncertain, let your error be toward too big rather than too small an outer skeleton.

Types of shipping crates

The kind of crate you would order to protect a picture in a simple frame destined to travel by truck a few hundred miles would not be the same as what you would want made to ship a clay vessel by freight across the continent. Plan the construction of your crate according to (1) the physical characteristics of what you are shipping, (2) the mode and exigencies of the proposed transportation, and (3) the duration and vagaries anticipated in its itinerary (see illustrative series #4).

Also take into consideration with all planned crates the human limitations of those who will receive them. Are you shipping to an institution where two able handymen are within call or only some elderly female volunteers? For you, it could be easier to pack six small sized objects in a single crate, but if its outer size and total weight are beyond the physical capacities of your recipients, personal health and the security of your shipment are better served by arranging for two or three lighter and smaller boxes. Too many accidents have happened to excellent crates because their construction was more than their unpackers could cope with.

Materials used to make crates

Excepting those sturdy monsters and elegant hand-crates (Fig 4) built to withstand the rigors of prolonged international travel or to afford accompanied care for great rarities, the majority of shipping crates designed for our services have wooden collars (their narrowest sides) combined with flat faces (their larger sides) of solid material (Fig 5). Open-slatted crates are prohibited for artifacts; they guarantee no protection for what they contain and invite damage. Solid materials employed for crate faces range from plywood, tongue-and-groove lumber, tempered masonite (and other forms of presd-wood), to soft rigid compositions like Celotex, Homosote

Fig 4. Here are two crate extremes: a small tailored hand-carrying case for an accompanying courier to use to transport a rare item by surface or air; next to it a large and weighty crate designed to contain multiple paintings destined for extended overseas exhibitions. Instructions for packers and examiners are adhered to the inner face of the opening lid; numbering and arrows indicate exact placement of each item; cushioning is attached to the crate itself; and to withstand repeated strains of opening and sealing, closings are metal, with inlaid receiving plates to accept sturdy bolts.

and sturdy paperboards. The soft rigid materials may only be employed for short-span truck travel as they do not withstand exposure to the elements or the grueling strains of trans-loading.

A wooden collar crate with masonite faces is adequate for shipping light-weight, reasonable-sized objects. Masonite holds up poorly under rough wear and tear and is so flexible it must always be reinforced with external cross-bracing in the wide dimension to prevent it from sagging inward. Whenever the largest dimension of a crate exceeds armspan or its weight exceeds the lifting ability of one person, external cross-braces (Fig 6) of three by one inch lumber strips secured to the narrower dimensions across a crate face—and often around its rim—are mandatory, even with tongue-and-groove wood construction. These braces also serve as hand-holds for moving personnel and help preclude "dumping" of your crate from its moving vehicle to the street beneath, from a freight car to a platform. On small but heavy crates the addition of flat-fitted metal handles (Fig 7) performs the same function. Remember, if you cannot handle your crate yourself on your own premises with reasonable security for its contents, time-conscious disinterested moving personnel beyond your sight are apt to treat it with angry abuse.

Directions for assembling a crate

Tell your carpenter he may use nails for building your crate but to deliver it to you with the closing lid separate, pre-drilled for screw attachment (Fig 8). Ask him to line all interior faces, including the top lid, with water-proof paper stapled or cemented in close contact. If the size of the crate demands external braces, these may be nailed in place before delivery, both on the bottom crate face and on its separate lid face. Whenever you and he have concluded that interior braces (Fig 9) will be employed to prevent shifting of contents, these should

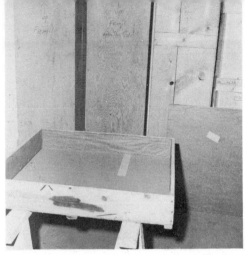

Fig 5. A customary shipping crate for artifacts. Separate lid is seen behind at the right. Both wooden collar and flat faces are lined with water-proof paper. The crate is ready for packing, placed on saw-horses to make the level for this work more convenient.

Fig 6. A sealed screw-top crate strengthened with external edge and crossbraces which will also serve as hand-holds for its movers. Ready for shipment, it bears opening information, symbol and legends of fragility, and its address label.

Fig 7. Side view of a small weighty crate showing one of its metal handles.

Fig 8. The main body of this sturdy crate is constructed with nails. Its closing lid has been pre-drilled and the screws are in place preparatory to sealing.

be made by the carpenter to exact measurements in advance and delivered to you, unattached, with the crate. Interior cross-braces are always positioned after contents is packed. They are secured, therefore, either from the outer or the inner face of a crate by screws only (Fig 10).

The logic of screws

A screw is inserted into place with a screw-driver; there is no shock, there is complete control. It should go into a pre-drilled hole of appropriate size. It goes where it is intended to go, its point does not bend and erupt in improper spaces. It is removed with a screw-driver, freeing an attachment without recourse to chisels, bar-wrenches, nail-pullers, or claw-hammers. Pre-drill-

Fig 9. A large heavy frame wrapped in Mylar and restrained from shifting within its tailored crate by interior crossbars, carefully secured with end blocks to the crate collar.

Fig 10. A detailed view of Fig 9 crate. All cushioning is adhered to the crate structure itself, the frame fits inside covered pads of rubber, the pads on the inner sides of the interior crossbraces compress against the frame front. This is an expensive, tailored crate, designed to transport an exceptionally heavy, valuable item, with complete cleanliness and utter security in packing, travel and unpacking.

ing holes to accept screws takes a little time. So does turning a screw-driver or a brace and bit (Fig 11). The safety factor far outweighs the time factor. Commercial firms refuse to accept this fact but no carpenter who has ever become concerned with crating valuables fails to appreciate the reasoning that requests screw attachment for any portion in or outside a crate AFTER its sensitive cargo has been positioned. If you will take a minute to consider that a single shipment must have its lid repositioned a minimum of four times on any loan, you will INSIST on prohibiting nails for this work.

The first screw-top crate you ever unpack yourself will convince you of the benefits for life.

Packing the object inside the crate

The best packing is always the simplest. Packing with too many peculiarities is unlikely to be duplicated by strangers. With no intent to insult, try to plan a foolproof packaging routine. Leave nothing to chance (see illustrative series #4). If you have disassembled an object, or packed multiple objects, LIST their total to be unpacked. Note down in order the different steps you took in any complex packaging, type these on a sheet, and staple their directions to the inner face of the closing lid and advise the borrower of the existence of these instructions. Taking the time and trouble to provide this information will be your best guarantee that your system

Fig 11. Using a brace and bit to secure screws in a closing lid. Note felt pencil for subsequent lettering of "OPEN THIS SIDE".

will be followed in repacking. Letters of instruction to a curator or director are excellent evidence of requested procedure but the person who receives them is not necessarily the same as the person who does the repacking. Do your utmost to reach that person directly.

Up-to-date packaging information

In our field we learn about new packing materials far too slowly. We remain consistently behind industry which is deeply concerned that its products reach purchasers in good state. Constant innovations are being mass-produced to assure the safe reception of delicate merchandise; packaging is an industry in itself. Although we could never risk untested use of all the new materials devised for commercial packing—too many might have deleterious chemical reactions in contact with our valuables—the knowledge of successful developments would improve our security and spare us wasted time and money.

Both the American Association of Museums and the American Association for State and Local History could help their membership if they were to include in their organizational publications bi-annual recommendations from packaging innovations. Some member of the editorial staffs could be asked to obtain and review packing data, request samples of those items which seemed serviceable and clear them for our use with a professional conservator. For what is passed on as safe, we should have information on sources of supply with full costs.

Right now we find new materials mostly by chance and with great difficulty as far as purchasing them goes. For example, a superior, flexible, tear-resistant waterproof paper was noted on a shipment of live plants; the nursery firm kindly obliged with the name and address of its supplier, but that firm proved utterly disinterested in selling its product except in vast bulk.

An official organizational inquiry, speaking as it would for a multitude of small customers, could reach beyond this impasse to locate an amenable sub-contractor. If all of us were informed every six months of what had been produced suitable to our requirements and where we could obtain this, annual membership fees for our organizations would become even better bargains.

Characteristics of interior packing materials

Each packing material has its peculiar function. The choice must be thoughtful. A customs official once unwrapped a synthetic covering from a painting where static electricity had caused close adhesion, and in so doing he pulled off islands of the varnish and paint. Immediate covering should isolate as well as protect a surface but should never cling to it, demanding force for its removal. Glazed and high-polish hard surfaces present few problems, but friable finishes, embroidered fabrics, beaded ornaments, painted, waxed, or lightly varnished surfaces must have initial wrappings which will not tend to adhere.

Also to be avoided in an initial wrapping is an "air-sealed" package, for this may trap moisture. An object impermeably enveloped in a warm room and then crated and sent out into frigid temperatures may get drenched within its air-tight envelope by the resulting condensation. The phenomenon of "Cargo Sweat" (which resembles what we experience wearing a plastic raincoat on a cold day) has plagued shippers of all materials. Objects thoughtlessly covered and transported through a range of climates have been known to develop such fluctuations of interior reactions to outside environments that tissue papers and fine cloths stuck so firmly to their surfaces that non-destructive removal could only be accomplished by skilled conservators. All interior packing requires a modicum of air circulation. It should eschew dust, litter, and all harmful deposits. It should be as simple to replace as to place—for what arrives in a box, within reason, should be expected to return with it.

Recommended interior packing materials

Glassine paper is optimum as an initial wrapping material for almost all objects. It is also one of the few recommended materials which is seldom reusable. Glassine paper (Fig 12) is translucent, rips easily, puckers harmfully if wetted, but has the ideal property of never adhering to dry varnish, waxed or other sensitive surfaces. Inexpensive, it may be purchased by the roll from artist material and paper supply firms. Standard types of glassine for our usage are the number 521, which is greenish in tone, 48 inches wide, and the number 522 which is greyish in tone and 42 inches wide. This material is safe to interleaf between unmounted prints and drawings, for wrapping textiles (also for padding the sharpness of their folds), and for direct wrapping of unframed paintings. In fact, use glassine with safety for the initial wrapping of any object with blunted form. It will not serve for pointed extremities, it rips too easily. Glassine offers no reliable exterior protection, only a very reliable INTERIOR isolation. Keep a minimum of two rolls on hand, use them freely, discard and replace the paper when torn; it is a valued expendable and should be viewed as such. Do not order glassine in quantities beyond foreseeable use; it embrittles with age, and anyway it is not difficult to obtain.

Where glassine has been used to supply isolation for a sensitive surface which might be damaged by the cling of static attraction, plastic sheetings are good secondary wrappings. Synthetic films are flexible, tough, water-resistant, and reusable. The majority are also air-fast and should never be completely sealed lest they trap moisture. All have marked static electricity and tend to adhere to non-isolated surfaces. Many plastic sheetings contain volatile components (smell is a practical test, if you are uncertain) and may disintegrate under extremes of temperatures. Some are incompatible for joining with self-adhesive tapes. The ordinary cellophanes, sold for gift wrappings, embrittle with age. For that matter so do many commercially available tissue papers. The danger of embrittlement is two-fold: an embrittled wrapping will break and cease to protect what it contains; an embrittled EDGE becomes knife-like. For those of you who have experienced the always surprising unpleasantness of a "paper cut" on flesh, the risk to delicate objects from stiff embrittlement and subsequent rupturing of a wrapping tissue is obvious. Any material which may serve to present a sharp cutting edge is no protection for an artifact.

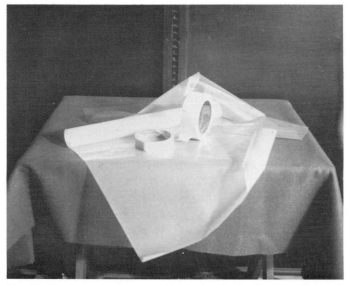

Fig 12. Photographed on a table in front of a lower wall easel, are a section of translucent glassine, on top of it two different widths of masking tape, and crumpled behind, a small piece of Mylar—transparent, tough, and flexible.

Among the plastic sheeting available for our use, Mylar (Fig 12) is highly recommended. This synthetic film has a powerful electrostatic charge but no volatile components and remains stable under both heat and cold. It is transparent, withstands repeated use, and has a long storage life. It may be joined firmly with self-adhesive tapes, emerging undamaged when these are pulled off. It offers excellent secondary protection for glassine wrapped objects and equally fine primary protection for non-friable surfaces. Mylar comes in a variety of thicknesses, identified by "mil" and "gauge", and oddly enough is sold by weight. Five pounds of gauge #100A, in either the 36 or 51 inch widths, will provide you with a reasonable supply. Mylar is expensive but despite its high cost you may find yourself reordering as you become acquainted with its superior protection and reusability. Mylar serves as dust covers for large items in storage, it may be hung as a curtain; wiped, washed clean; creasing, handling abuse, even stapling wear it out only slowly; you will find yourself reluctant to part with any piece of Mylar, sections of which may still be useful.

Fillers and padding

All cushioning shock-absorbers used in packing which are free form fillers are litter makers. Occasionally pressures of time, shortage of funds, and difficulty in obtaining better substitutes force us to employ these but none of them is without unfortunate packing characteristics. By far the worst is excelsior and excelsior padding. The pads break easily. Free excelsior has sharp points, worms its way into any crack, seam or joint, scratches and cuts surfaces, embeds itself in paint and varnish, and is difficult, often dangerous, to remove. Excelsior is both a fire-hazard and a retainer of moisture. Crates packed with excelsior padding and shipped in zero temperatures have been opened to reveal sopping

Fig 13. Between two different types of aircap sheeting is a small rolled piece of Kimpak, one corner pulled apart to show its laminated composition.

wet contents. The material in either free or padded form is inexpensive and readily supplied by commercial movers (and as readily employed by them) but it is bad.

Expanded and exploded plastics are not needle-sharp and some are fire-proofed, but to normal litter-making they add their electrostatic nuisance of clinging to everything and everybody in their vicinity. Unpack a delicate sculpture cushioned with one of these fillers and you will go out of your way never to repeat the nightmare.

Papier-machè-filled padding breaks less readily than excelsior pads and its filler is not sharp-edged but is very dirt and dust producing. The best paper padding is the crepe-paper filled form. Kimpak (Fig 13), one of these, comes in wide rolls, easily cut to size for use, offering very limited leakage from the filling and few damaging factors. Kimpak may be stapled or taped and is reasonably reusable. It does not appear to attract appreciable moisture and serves well for both wrapped padding and space filling. A carton (about $30) will last you a long time and not deteriorate in storage.

Aircap plastic sheetings (Fig 13) are expensive, absolutely clean, fine cushioning, fairly reusable (though people cannot seem to resist the temptation to "pop" their bubbles) and such a recent innovation that un-

Fig 14. Cloth covered sponge plastic pads firmly secured in their designed positions on a tailored crate. The waterproof lining here is sisal Kraft paper, used by construction firms, advisedly cemented to the inside rather than stapled due to its soft tar content which should never leak out over the inner faces. This material comes in many widths and is excellent.

packers regard them with awe, according an equal respect for what they protect. Do not use these over the face of a painting without an initial wrapping in glassine. They offer good protection for carved and perforated frames in small dimensions. Should your borrower want an ivory miniature, a rare timepiece, or a unique patchwork quilt, packing with aircap wrappings is guaranteed to elicit extra care for your treasure from his hands.

Soft and firm plastic and rubber sponges, thick sections of hemp (such as undercarpeting) and webbed sisal, may be used as filling pads. But for all which shed their particles, cloth envelopes are advisable (Fig 14). Few of these materials should ever come in direct contact with your valuables and then only with such solid exteriors as hard wood or stone. Cloth wrapped, their resiliency makes effective cushioning which can be solidly adhered to the insides of a crate, tailored to receive an exact form (Fig 15 and 16). Both synthetic and rubber sponges deteriorate under temperature extremes, losing their original properties of compression and expansion; cloth coverings do not prevent this change but they prohibit any spill of the altered contents.

Slabs of expanded polystyrene foam have been successfully cut and trimmed to fit exact proportions of delicate figurines with non-friable finishes. This takes time and skill. It also requires elaborate repacking instructions to avoid confusion. Intricate arrangements of such fitted slabs have to be applied and removed by the lettered number but they restrain and cushion neatly. Since this material is light, firm, and shed-resistant, it is ideal for packing valuables to be shipped by air express (Fig 17). Unlike the soft sponge plastics, polystyrene slabs are unaffected by normal temperature ranges. However, they have little "give" and when employed as space fillers must fit exactly or they cannot be relied on to prevent contents shifting.

Easily obtainable white tissue papers, Butcher paper,

Fig 15. A view of the whole crate (Fig 14) and part of its closing lid, recessed to provide tightness of fit. This is an expensive tailored crate designed to transport a single framed painting of very great value.

Fig 16. The same crate with the glassine-wrapped framed painting fitted into its receiving cushions, face up. Cushions on the closing lid are planned to provide exact pressure for complete control of contents in transit. At the request of the insurance company, this crate was shipped under the Special Fine Arts Contract of REA insured for 10% of its full valuation, separately covered by its own Fine Arts All Risk policy. No damage occurred.

Fig 17. Trimmed slabs of polystyrene were the rim fillers and aircap sheeting was the inner wrapping for a small rare artifact shipped in a light-weight screw-top crate via air express under protective signature. No damage.

brown Kraft paper, or waxed paper, all serve in emergencies but provide inferior protection (especially in regard to the dangers of their cutting edges) to the recommended materials. Self-adhesive tapes are always advisable for holding wrappings secure; string and cloth tapes both act to cut into wrappings and present acute lines of pressure against the contents. Masking or decorator tapes are more visible and easier to free than transparent self-adhesive tapes. The removal of these tapes will tear glassine paper, tissue paper, and to a lesser extent Butcher, Kraft, wax papers, Kimpak, and aircap sheeting. Their removal will not tear Mylar. If you use small sections of tape to secure glassine, the rip-off damage is only slight. Unpacking will teach you a lot about packing.

Purchase and storage of packing materials

Many of the described materials, including Mylar, may be obtained from the mail order catalogues of Sears Roebuck and Montgomery Ward. Prompt delivery is not always assured as special items like these are often out of stock but these sources of supply are accessible to everyone. Accommodating hardware stores occasionally will oblige as an intermediary purchaser, re-selling materials to you which the producer will not sell direct. Sales taxes have much to do with manufacturer's refusal to ship to a final consumer. If you combine your purchasing with neighboring colleagues the cost and delivery of supplies improve in proportion to the total amounts ordered.

Storage of packing materials presents a real problem. If you lend as seldom as six times a year you still cannot afford the expense of time and energy to locate supplies needed for each individual shipment. Practical economy stipulates purchasing in slight excess of any immediate needs. Advisably you should keep on hand two rolls of glassine paper, one roll of Mylar, and a roll of Kimpak

Fig 18. An undertable storage cart made of metal lumber (Dexion) and equipped with casters. Pipe sections hold rolled supplies, compartments with plywood bottoms hold other supplies. Sturdy, heavy, but easily moved.

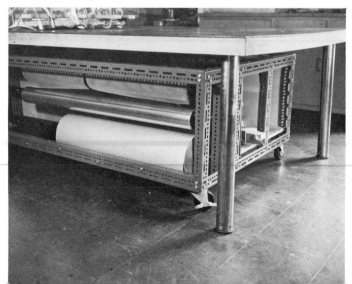

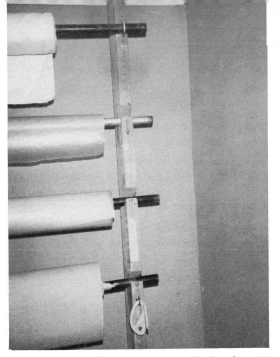

Fig 19. Section of a wall storage rack, showing one of its solid 2″ x 6″ uprights, slotted to receive the pipe sections on which rolled supplies may be stored.

for minimum recourse. WHERE can you keep these? Institutions large and small are constantly hamstrung for lack of space, let alone convenient space. One method is to store packing supplies under your work table on moveable carts (Fig 18) designed to fit this space and equipped with pieces of pipes to hold the rolls. Another is to erect a wall storage rack on any bare wall in an attic or dry basement (Fig 19). Either system requires slight cost and labor but does provide convenient accessibility for what you need when you need it. Under-table storage consumes no extra space; wall storage consumes, as a rule, space which was previously unused.

Final considerations on packing your collection for travel

When you have finished packing an object inside a crate, you should be able to jar the crate and observe no evidence (or sound!) of movement. A light object, centered within filler packing, will only remain secure against shock if the padding is firmly stuffed in. A heavy object is more likely to shift inside a crate than a light object and therefore demands more rigid forms of restraint. Interior braces only eliminate hazards of motion when they press down firmly against an already wrapped or padded object. Whatever is loosely packed is not safely packed; all contacts should be firm but never exert undue strains. Do not expect more from your selected packing materials than their physical characteristics can provide. Strongly compressed Kimpak pads will not return to their original thickness in the same way that cloth-covered rubber sponge will (until it has aged too much!). Torn glassine should always be replaced with fresh. There is a limitation to the effective reuse of self-adhesive tapes. Exhausted materials of all types cannot serve their original function any more than a bar of rust can substitute for its initial iron. Certain attempts to economize in packing and shipping historic and artistic works turn out to be tragically expensive.

The outside of your crate

Attach the lid of your crate with a screw which has length and thickness appropriate to the dimension of the crate. Take your carpenter's advice on this since, as he will tell you, the pre-drilled holes are made to the size of the ROOT diameter of the selected screw and not to its THREAD diameter. Pilot holes of root diameter permit the threads of your screw to grip all along their length and hold down the closing lid hard and fast. On large crates which require long and thick screws, predrilling into the crate collar may be necessary and if so, should be done by your carpenter. A brace and bit, an electric screw-driver, soaping the screw ends in advance, will help make the final attachment easier for you. If you feel unable to perform this task yourself, supervise it. Remember, you must rely on the word, intelligence, concern, and sense of responsibility of everyone who performs any part of your packing beyond the range of your eagle eye. This is not automatically identical with your standards.

After your crate has been screwed closed, take a felt pencil or a fat dark crayon and letter neatly on the top face, "OPEN THIS SIDE" (Fig 6), have someone help you turn the crate to its opposite face and there letter "OPEN OTHER SIDE". This is not redundant. Too few people are accustomed to screw-top crate fastening and many a receiver has wrecked a beautifully prepared shipment by ripping off the wrong face to get at the contents. NEVER omit this precaution.

Warning symbols and legends on the exterior of a crate elicit attention to its vulnerable contents, not perhaps as thorough attention as could be desired but unquestionably more care in handling than would be accorded without them. The international mark for fragility is a broken wine glass (Fig 20). You might be able to locate a stencil for this but cutting one on your own is no great chore. For the words "FRAGILE," "HANDLE WITH CARE," or "WORKS OF ART," the use of metal stencil alphabets (Fig 21) offer speed, ease and repeated use. All warnings are best applied in red paint. Apply those you prefer. The most potent are the broken wine glass and "Handle with care" Arrows indicating top and bottom of a crate may also be included, but will not act to prevent the uninformed from attempting to open the wrong face.

Do not spread addresses over the face of a crate; it has to be returned to you. Obliterating one extensive

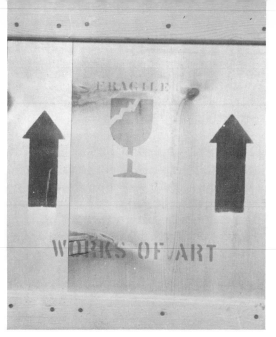

Fig 20. Legends and symbol of fragility stenciled on the outside of a crate. The arrows are usually applied to indicate preferred positioning during travel.

set of directions and substituting another in its place can create the appearance and confusion of a kindergarten blackboard. Exterior shipping directions should be inscribed on a label, glued or stapled (Fig 22) to the face of the opening lid of a crate. These are easily washed off and replaced, or covered, for return directions and concentrate the attention of a reader. A sound practice is to prepare your own return shipping label, securing same with masking tapes behind a sheet of Mylar to the inner face of the closing lid, right next to your page of packing instructions. If you include all specifics of shipment desired (mode of transportation requested, valuation, "Protective Signature Service," etc.) you provide the best assurance that these will be met on the way home.

Fig 21. This stencil for the broken wine glass was home-made. The legends are formed from metal stencil alphabets.

Ways to ship

Depending on size, weight, and occasionally contents, valuable objects may be shipped via United States Mail (definite limitations by law), Railway Express Agency (not what it once was!), air freight and air express (varied limitations and classifications), rail freight (very much not what it once was!), trucking firms (direct and transfer systems), and institutional vans (only the wealthy possess these). The most important consideration is whether the proposed transportation guarantees door to door delivery or whether your shipment must be delivered to and collected from some depot. Today, no form of transportation is totally faultless. Neither expense of selected mode of travel nor a plethora of special contracts can promise complete security for collection shipments. One of the more reliable influential factors in

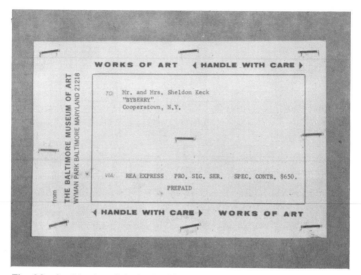

Fig 22. A shipping label of stiff paper, clear, concise and easy to replace. This example is a printed form but a typed plain label is equally effective.

arranging transportation is still individual experience with a particular firm or with its personnel.

The reliance on trucking firms for transporting artifacts increases steadily for long as well as short hauls. Truck firms vary in their performances. Good ones have the dual accompaniment of "relief drivers" on their vehicles. A vehicle left unattended at rest or emergency stops is subject to looting, and some have been. Reputable truckers also assure a shipper that when delivery is rendered impossible due to unforeseen time factors, the shipment remains secured under lock and cover until such moment as delivery can be made. Too many crates have been found dumped outside a temporarily closed building. Demand person to person transportation with receipts signed by accredited personnel. Also make sure the truck transport is a closed van and not an open one covered with tarpaulin. Good truck firms are excellent, poor ones are unbelievably awful and both often proffer the same advertisements of their services.

Insurance

Your biggest asset in choosing a policy to cover the value of your collection in transit is an intelligent and concerned insurance agent. Both adjectives have equal importance. On all loans, the policy should protect you as well as the borrower. Policies must often be adjusted from their general format to suit the nature of the material shipped, the mode for its travel, and the extent of the itinerary. Many insurance policies are void if an item is shipped outside contiguous portions of the United States. Irrespective of what insurance guarantees are made by your selected common carrier, recommended coverage is a separate Fine Arts All Risk policy for full valuation of the object or objects involved.

Appraisal of value is a ticklish business. An insurance company may be willing to sell you a policy for any valuation you choose to place on your object, but nevertheless, in case of claim for loss or damage you will find the burden of justifying this evaluation rests on you. Get supporting evidence for monetary appraisals. Resort to professional appraisers—if these are acceptable to your insurance agent—or estimates of value from an authority who could command legal respect. If you can locate no outside help for evaluation, refer to prices in current auction catalogues for items similar to yours; you may still be required to prove the authenticity of your comparison in case of controversy but so will the other side. Do not neglect to insure frames, stands, and peripheral accessories to an object when these have independent value, and put them down for full replacement costs. Turn back a few pages and notice that the damage illustrated (Fig 2) which did not harm the painting did break its frame.

Follow your agent's advice. It is to his interest to

protect you. Should your claim for loss or accident reach a court of law, he is better equipped to handle its presentation than you are. On items valued in the $100,000 category some insurance companies require the additional expense of special contract forms from your carriers. The Special Fine Arts Contract of REA, for example, very costly per unit of weight, gives you small protection in itself but the inclusion of this frill at its lower figures does provide your insurance company adjustor an opportunity for subrogation in event of claim and acts to benefit his position. Comply with your agent's requests especially when large sums are the price of replacing treasures.

All common carriers have liability limitations on their monetary responsibility for everything they move. These are regulated by law. Private individuals are not subject to such regulations. When you move any object or crated objects in a private vehicle, notify your insurance agent of your intent and find out if you are covered or need an extra form of protection against loss or accident. Unless you take this precaution, you could become enmeshed in an unpleasant private lawsuit to collect for a claim. A van which is legally the property of an institution is covered by normal insurance policies.

Remember that the borrower pays crating, shipping, and insurance fees. Choose the best. You are the travel agent for your collection.

Record photography of damages

The borrower should not be expected to pay costs for photography. This is an expense which you should accept and incur. Your pre-shipment photograph—and don't let its negatives out of your hand—records the condition of your loan as it left your possession. It is legal statement of a "before" which one anticipates will not be altered by travel. However, accidents can and do occur.

Should a crate arrive in an obvious state of disruption, photograph its appearance if you possibly can before you dismantle it. You may find the contents undamaged, but if not, you are collecting primary evidence toward determining responsibility for the recompense of your claim. When you find the contents damaged (Fig 2) with or without external warnings of this sorry fact, beg, borrow, or steal to have it photographed at once. Take as many photographs as you will need to illustrate the extent and nature of the damage. Make plenty of prints and hang on to their negatives.

Report any claim for damage or loss immediately both to your insurance agent and to the sender. Insurance policies have a time limit (this varies) for admissibility of claim. Never delay and never rely on word of mouth communications. All you need to prove is that your possession was damaged or lost while you were covered for protection against this, and that the monetary recompense you claim is legally justified. Type your statement of claim (keep a carbon copy) and send with it your evidence of prior condition and present condition (or loss). Your dated pre-shipment photograph and dated record-of-damage photograph pinpoint the period of time during which the accident occurred. It is the business of the insurance company's agents and adjustors to pinpoint the cause of damage and the responsible payee.

Until you have gone through the experience of collecting for a claim, you will not appreciate how simple this can be under prepared circumstances of surety and how heart-breakingly litigation can stretch out into utter disillusion when there is no positive evidence to confirm the accuracy of your contention. Perfectly justified claims for serious damage to rare works of art have gone unrecompensed because owners were ignorant of how they could have protected, photographically, both their purse and their treasure. With irrefutable photographic records even small claims receive instant settlement. A good insurance agent will work for your benefit but without supporting documentation he cannot get the best possible settlement of your claim. Make record photography a steady habit. You will never regret : the expense.

Conclusion

If all the foregoing suggestions and advice seem fulsome and more than you are prepared to face, then you had better establish a policy of not lending. There are people who never undertake voyages because they cannot face the onus of getting passports, vaccinations, tickets, reservations, and dread the thought of strange discomforts in unfamiliar environments. Cultural artifacts are inanimate: they can take no steps in self-defense. Either those, by whose powers of decision they are sent forth to endure the rigors of travel, plan for their protection, or, like orphans in a storm, their prospects for survival are a matter of sheer chance.

In one sense lending is publicity promotion. Distant viewers who see an interesting object often learn of its home base for the first time; others may decide that if this piece is typical of the quality of a collection they would like to visit the whole. Much of the value of lending depends on where and how an item is displayed. In every case, it should always reflect credit on its owner. An object of great inherent merit, displayed in sad physical state, shipped in sub-standard procedures, arouses sympathy for itself and disrespect for its owner. Do not lend unless you are willing to do it well.

Once you have been initiated into the travel circuit you will recognize that the information presented here is anything but excessive. It is no more than was indicated: it offers only prior knowledge on what to expect, what to forestall, and how to protect your historical material and your investment in it. Beyond doubt implementation of its information implies expense. Consider that the costs for proper working equipment, photographic installation, storage racks for supplies, are all one-time expenses. Estimate that except for photographic supplies and photo-processing (and staff TIME), all other costs are for expendables (crates, packing materials, insurances) for which you will be reimbursed by the borrower. Weigh the importance and value of your collection and your reputation. If you decide to lend, you will have to include some costs for the activity in your budget. You cannot afford to do otherwise.

Sources of additional information

As was stated in the beginning, the intent of this publication is to simplify and clarify the basic requirements for safeguarding your collection in travel. Instructions, procedures, materials, have all been kept at a minimum in an effort to concentrate attention on the general principles involved.

Countless complications are not even mentioned. As you encounter unfamiliar problems, you will need assistance to work out your own solutions of these. The following three references have been selected because they deal with much that you already know but in more sophisticated detail. Buy them if possible.

MUSEUM REGISTRATION METHODS, Dudley and Wilkinson, revised ed. 1968 published by the American Association of Museums and the Smithsonian Institution.

Granted much of the information in this book does not apply to small organizations, nowhere can you find better advice and directions for dealing with the countless headaches you never suspected could exist.

A PRIMER ON MUSEUM SECURITY, Keck, Block, Chapman, Lawton & Stolow, 1966. published by (and available from) The New York State Historical Association.

Dr. Stolow's explanations of environment and light factors will help you justify to your board of trustees loan refusals you judge wise. The chapter on insurance can help both you and your agent to draft policies adjusted to special protections you want. Some of the other information will be more details on what you already know.

THE MURRAY PEASE REPORT and CODE OF ETHICS FOR ART CONSERVATORS 1968, published by the International Institute for Conservation of Historic and Artistic Works, American Group. Available (price $1.00) from the Conservation Center, Institute of Fine Arts, 1 East 78th Street, New York.

Of importance to you in this pamphlet is the description of standard work and relationship practices. It will provide you with an official yardstick for your judgment on the professional competence of experts you may consider employing and confirm the quality of performance which you are entitled to receive.

New York State Historical Association   Loan Data Sheet

No.   Title

Artist   Period or date

Insurance valuation
Outgoing to   Date requested

Incoming from   Date received

Shipment received via   Insured by
                       Crate
Shipment to be made via   Insured by

To be wrapped
To be crated   Measurement for crating: Height   Width   Thickness

Watercolor	Painting	Pastel	Black&White	Other
on masonite	on wood	on paper	on fabric	on cardboard
other				
Unframed	Framed	Condition of frame		
Glazed	Taped	Plexiglas	Warning against tape	
Backing	of wood	of board	other	
	condition of backing			
Stripping	of wood	of metal		

Secured to frame with metal straps   with nails   other
Label attached to prevent removal from frame   label intact

Pictograph:

Treatment required prior to loan   postponed
        to artifact
        to frame   completed

Preliminary examination made by   Date
Examination on return made by   Date
Description of insurance claim if any

Percentage of depreciation if any

BERNICE P. BISHOP MUSEUM
HONOLULU, HAWAII 96819

SHIPPING INVOICE

TO

Our Invoice No. **BP — 2426**
Show this number on all shipments, invoices and correspondence.

Your Invoice No.

Shipping date

Via

Prepaid Collect

Contained in

PURPOSE

Loan at your request
For identification
Open exchange
In exchange for

Return of material sent for identification
Return of material we borrowed
Gift
Other

Recommended by
Signature

Registrar
Signature

In connection with material sent on loan: This loan is made for a period of . Extension of the period may be granted only when permission is requested in writing *prior* to the expiration date. *All* specimens must be returned except those that the Bishop Museum authorizes you to keep.

QUANTITY	NAME OF SPECIMEN	ORIGIN	COLLECTOR	IDENT. NO.

Please return this material to: THE BISHOP MUSEUM, Dept. of
1355 Kalihi St., Honolulu, Hawaii 96819, U. S. A.
Ship by: Parcel Post Prepaid Express Other

Please SIGN and RETURN this form promptly to
The Registrar, BISHOP MUSEUM
1. 1355 Kalihi Street P. O. Box 6037
Honolulu, Hawaii 96819 U. S. A.

Received in good condition Except as noted
Signature
Position Date

BPB Reg. Form No. 101 May 20, 1968

Bernice P. Bishop Museum
PAINTINGS EXAMINATION FORM   Accession No. _____ Ptg. No._____

Priority 1 2 3 / BM 1 2 3   Location_____

Artist _____ Title _____
Date painted _____ Related paintings _____
Signature _____ Sig. location_____
Size: Sight/Stretcher: Height _____ Width _____ Shape _____
Date examined _____ Examined by _____ In ___ Out___ Frame
Casual _____ Complete _____ Materials used _____
****
Stretcher type & remarks

Support
fabric   acad. board   lined   cradled
wood   presdwood   brittle   hole
paper   glass   sagging   tear
paperboard   other   draws   dent

Medium
oil   pastel   mixture
watercolor   tempera   other

Ground and paint film
abraded   cupping   powdering
buckling   flaking   scratches
cleavage   losses   other

Surface coating
varnished   grime   crazed varnish
unvarnished   bloom   fingermarks
glass   scratches   other

Framing
framed   unframed, frame stored   poor backing
damaged frame   unframed, frame missing   separation
held with nails   transcribe info on frame   screw eyes
touching glass   no backing

Previous treatment evidence

****
Photography: photograph later_____ b&w_____ color _____
Old_____ Neg. No._____Date _____ Filed _____
Current_____ Neg. No._____Date _____ Filed _____
Picture details*********************************Back details*********************
Examination indicates: treatment urgent   soon   not needed
a. major treatment   to surface   to frame   to backing
b. minor treatment   to structure   to support   to mount

Remarks:

Illustrative Series

A WALL EASEL PREPARED FOR YOUR
PRE-SHIPPING RECORD PHOTOGRAPHY

If an inexpensive artist's easel is cannibalized and its service members firmly adhered to a free wall (Fig 1), the resulting installation offers permanent solidity and occupies a minimum of space in a room employed for activities other than photography. Painting the wall a flat black will eliminate reflections, and installing a double electric base plug directly beneath the easel upright will avoid dangers from long extension cords. Camera, tripod, and photographic lights can be brought here when needed (Fig 2). The only other consideration is being able to clear space, temporarily, in front of the wall easel on occasion of its use for photography.

The wall easel illustrated (Fig 3) is equipped for conservation record photography of paintings. Among its added accessories, pertinent for you are the open-topped plastic pockets, here either side of the Kodak grey and color scale on the lower moveable easel member, but which could extend a wider distance. Identification data written with white ink on black paper can be inserted into these with the aid of a jeweler's tweezers (Fig 4) and their information included in the photographic exposure. In the example shown the painting's identity number and code symbol to indicate stage in treatment are being included. You could include your museum's acquisition number and the date of exposure.

For object photography, place a table against the wall, lower the easel members below its level, and print your data on a stiff dark card, propped up adjacent to the object and within the photographic confines.

The slight expense and effort involved in preparing a stationary easel with a transparent information pocket on its lower bar is amply repaid by the ease with which you can produce irrefutable evidence of physical state recorded at a given date.

54

Fig. 1

Fig. 2

Fig. 3

Fig. 4

A METHOD FOR PACKING A FRAMED PAINTING IN A CRATE

(Photographs reproduced permission of the Baltimore Museum of Art)

The following photographic series was made at the author's request by the Baltimore Museum of Art, courtesy of their conservation department. In my opinion, this museum does uniformly good packing and shipping at a reasonably inexpensive level. Their packer is an expert in care and planning; the steps in the progress of his work here may give you good suggestions. This is a re-used crate, not one tailored especially to receive a particular item. The only fault I find with this kind of packing is that it presumes similar intelligence and skill on the part of the repacker. If you know the quality of your recipient, there is no problem; but if his packing is uninformed and sub-standard there is small chance that the item will be accorded equal protection on its return trip!

1. The packer's supply bench is adjacent to the long packing table (extending from the far left) and in all the times I have visited this room, unannounced, I have never seen it in other than apple-pie order.

2. This is the packing table; the supply bench is at the far end, top of this picture. The framed painting has passed inspection of its physical state, security within its frame (edge stripping, protective backing, metal plate screw attachment to its frame) and attention is now directed to the areas of vulnerability on the frame. Note padding on which item rests, eliminating danger of slipping during work.

3. All protruding carved forms on a frame, especially those with openings, require interlaced cushioning (with strips of Kimpak, soft synthetic sponge, or cotton wadding) to keep them undamaged.

4. Any delicate ornamentation left UNPRO-TECTED is apt to be missing, broken or cracked on the return from travel. (Many museums remove elaborate frames and substitute simple moulding travel frames for loans).

5. Composite arrangements of soft center and outer sturdy padding can be made to accommodate center sections of corner carvings.

6. Frame corners suffer the greatest abuse in handling and travel. The first padding is placed against their sides.

7. The prepared top padding is positioned.

8. Secured in place with masking tapes.

9. The ends of the sturdy outer padding are turned over to the reverse of the frame and stapled to it for firm security.

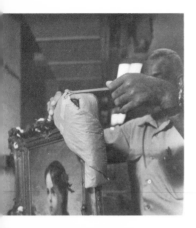

10. Since staples may work loose in shipment and, free-floating, become deadly hazards, additional masking tape is used to cover their heads and adhere to them.

11. When all the ornaments and corners are completely padded, both the painting and its frame are supplied with immediate shock absorbers.

12. A clean cardboard, cut to measure, is fitted into the bottom of the waterproof lined crate. This is an additional form of protection, related to the fact that the crate is not tailored but a re-used container as further steps will indicate.

13. On top of this cardboard the padded framed painting is placed face down, and centered in the crate.

14. On every side the excess space between the padded painting and the inner face of the crate collar is blocked with cushioning pads until the fit is tight.

15. A second cardboard, cut to measure, is placed over the packed painting.

16. Two interior braces of light wood provided with flat end blocks for secure attachment and made to exact measure are placed in position. These serve to compress the cardboard firmly against the padded frame and prevent any shifting of the contents in the depth dimension. In this instance the braces are essential because the re-used crate is deeper than necessary for the dimension of its contents.

17. Interior braces are always secured into their flat end blocks with screws and the location of the screwheads clearly indicated with circles of red or black crayon. Here, the screws are being applied from the outer face of the crate collar; they may also be applied on its interior, but SCREWS must always be used to facilitate a harmless placement and removal of the braces.

18. The closing lid, secured with screws and reinforced with crossbraces externally applied in advance, lined with waterproof paper on its inner face, shows the marks of its prior usages. Former directions must all be painted out before the new shipping label will be visibly isolated as a current instruction to the shipper.

A METHOD FOR CONSTRUCTING A BOX AND PACKING A BOXED ITEM

(photographs reproduced permission of the Baltimore Museum of Art)

This series, demonstrated by the expert packer of the Baltimore Museum of Art, illustrates both the steps in preparing and making an interior box, and in adjusting a re-used crate where the depth is appropriate for its contents but the width and length are too great. The remodeled crate will hold two boxed items although we observe the boxing of only one of these. Glazed prints and paintings in narrow or "strip" (as seen here) frames are best protected by boxing prior to packing. Items in unfoliated deep frames may be boxed; when the depth of the frame provides space to prohibit any danger of immediate contact with packing materials this is not essential. Small multiple-part and delicate objects are also advisably boxed before packing in a crate. Boxing affords extra travel precaution and invites concentrated attention from an unpacker.

7. The sides of the box must equal the thickness of the wrapped painting; this must be measured carefully and take into consideration the entire thickness as it exists.

8. The outer extremities of the box are drawn too.

9. Once the whole pattern has been outlined, the painting is removed and the exterior limits cut out, the interior folds incised for ease in bending.

10. Here is the cut-out box, all folding sections pre-bent, ready for service.

11. The glassine-wrapped painting is placed face down in the box center and the sides of the box brought into place.

12. The final sections meet perfectly. (You will not succeed this well on your first attempt but by your third you will be fairly expert.)

13. The fitted box is sealed with masking tapes.

14. The sealed box is wrapped in waterproof paper.

15. This is sealed with masking tapes. (The second painting was similarly boxed.)

16. The selected used crate has proper depth for the two paintings but is otherwise far too large. It is lined with waterproof paper.

17. The correct area to confine the two boxed paintings is measured off and divider sections are nailed and cemented into place to provide this. These dividers are made of light wood, their firm security reinforced with carefully provided end blocks.

18. Here is the packing space to be used with the first boxed painting in place about to be covered with a cardboard divider between the boxes. Padding around the edges is less than with an unboxed item since the boxing provides extra resiliency.

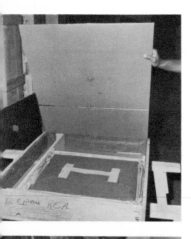

19. Second boxed painting in position with its rim padding, cover cardboard for this seen at left, and behind crate the cardboard used to cover the entire interior space of the crate. Note how crate depth is exactly adequate for the two boxed items plus the interleaving cardboards and permits no danger of contents shifting.

20. I would judge that after this crate was originally packed, its external state was considered inadequate and that it was unpacked and the extra corner blocks secured to brace the structure. Here it is shown packed to satisfaction with the cover lid being screwed down. Provided all the dimensions have been accurately figured, packing boxed items is very simple.

21. The packed re-used crate, an economical and intelligent adjustment completed with all reasonable precautions for travel. Note the necessity for painting out all the previous addresses so that the current set of directions will be clear; had labels been employed previously, these would only have had to be soaked off and replaced with a fresh one, eliminating the necessity for the splotched appearance.

PACKING A FRAGILE OBJECT FOR OVERSEAS LOAN
(Photographs reproduced permission of The New York State Historical Association)

This early American windmill figure is rare and fragile. When it was requested by the United States Government for exhibition at the Tokyo World's Fair, the loan was authorized only after the borrower agreed to pay full costs of a tailored travel crate. There are three separate parts to the figure's exhibition: the figure proper (with the blades at rest extending BELOW the level of the feet); the metal rod which holds the figure erect and raises it above its base (unfortunately not visible in the photograph of the figure); and the base itself.

This crate was packed and unpacked several times until the set of directions for the work was as concise and direct as could be stated. On the final packing, each portion was color coded: the portion of the inner crate holding the figure was painted one color; the portion to hold the base, painted another; the slot to receive the metal rod painted still another. Two sets of these packing photographs with their text were prepared; one accompanied the crate, in an envelope secured to the inner lid; the other was forwarded to the exhibition director.

The plan for packing was kept as simple as possible. There are no excess materials involved, everything which comes in the crate goes back with it. The weight of the crate was above customary for its size and its construction additionally bolstered with corner and edge additions; it had to withstand loading and reloading far beyond that presumed for continental travel. The entire plan of the crate and of its packing took into consideration the problems presented by the object, the circumstances anticipated in its trip, and the hope that the unpacker and repacker would find their work simple and comprehensible.

71

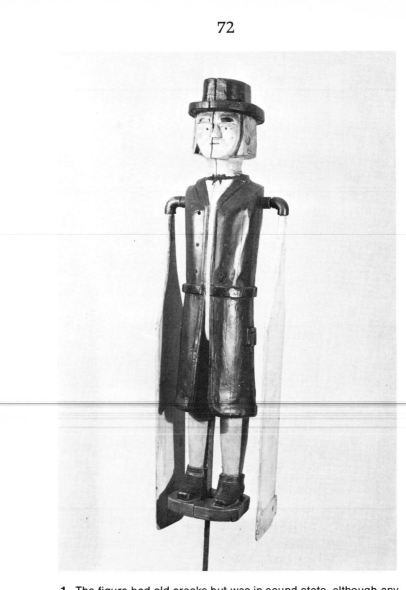

1. The figure had old cracks but was in sound state, although any misunderstanding manipulation was hazardous. Unless the blade arms were positioned horizontally it could not stand upright except on its metal rod and stand. The metal rod could be unscrewed from both the base and the figure. The figure could therefore be packed with its exhibition accessories separated.

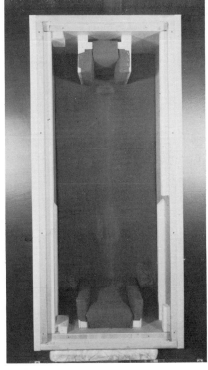 

2. The case was lined with waterproof paper and this in turn was covered with felt. The receiving pockets for the figure were designed to its form and cushioned with felt covered sponge. Measurements were exact and padding was planned for a firm fit.

3. The figure was gently eased into its cushioned pockets.

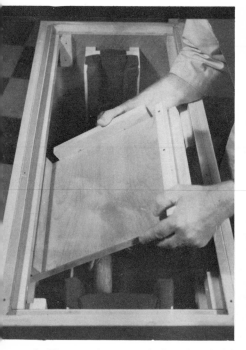

4. The wooden tray, designed to hold the base into which the metal rod fitted, was slipped into a slot prepared to receive it.

5. And settled into place against the rim planned to receive it on the opposite side.

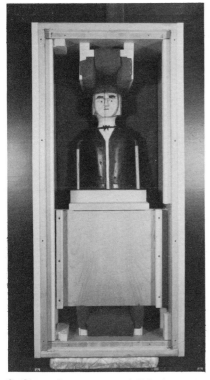

6. Since the reverse of this tray was padded, when it was fitted into place it served to secure the lower portion of the figure against vertical movement.

7. The wooden base was placed in the prepared tray.

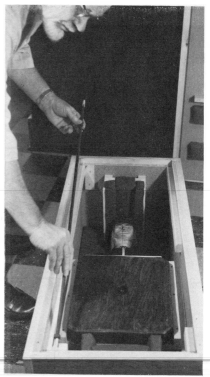

8. It rests there, hole side up, emphasizing its relationship to the figure.

9. The metal rod is placed in the side slot prepared to receive it.

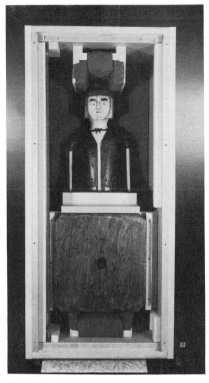

10. Note the two small blocks which restrain this rod within the crate to prevent any side slippage.

11. The lid of the crate, recessed at its edges to fit exactly over the slot holding the metal bar, has wooden blocks and felt covered pads placed to restrain the packed base.

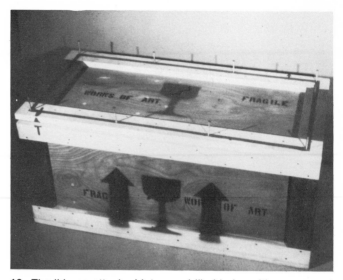

12. The lid was attached into pre-drilled holes with screws and the outer face of the crate decorated with travel symbols of fragility. Note small arrow at the left to indicate exact positioning of the lid for the re-packer.